Scottish Maritime 1600-1850

A Guide for Family Historians

by David Dobson

CLEARFIELD

Originally published
St. Andrews, Fife, Scotland, 1996

Reprinted for Clearfield Company, Inc., by
Genealogical Publishing Co., Inc.
Baltimore, Maryland
1997, 1999, 2010

ISBN 978-0-8063-4717-2

Made in the United States of America

SCOTTISH MARITIME RECORDS 1600-1850

INTRODUCTION

Seafaring was, and continues to be, of importance to an island nation such as Scotland. When one considers the relevance of seafaring to Scottish society and the economy over the centuries it does not seem improbable that some, at least, of our ancestors were engaged in that industry. The liklihood increases when one takes into account the fact that the majority of Scotland's population has traditionally lived in close proximity to the sea.

Having worked through vital data sources such as the statutory records of births, marriages and deaths, the census returns, and the contents of the Old Parish Registers and established a maritime connection, where does one turn next? The Society of Genealogists' *"My Ancestor was a Merchant Seaman. How can I find out more about him?"* is a useful publication, especially if one is researching a seafaring ancestor of the Victorian period or later. The object of this book is provide a Scottish source book for the period between 1600 and 1850, which identifies the range of sources available and where relevant information both published and manuscript can be located within Scotland.

SCOTTISH MARITIME RECORDS

ROYAL NAVY

In the time between the Union of the Crowns of Scotland and England in 1603 until the Union of the Parliaments of 1707 there was little need for the Scottish Government to maintain a separate navy. A minimal naval power existed which could be rapidly expanded during periods of warfare by impressing merchant vessels and their crews and by licencing privateers to harass the enemy's shipping.

Scotland's traditional foe, England, now became de facto the protecting power, with the result that the historic allies of Scotland, especially the French and the Dutch, became from time to time Scotland's enemies. English naval vessels were to be found carrying out duties in Scottish waters in support of the government in Edinburgh, and indirectly the government in London, despite occasional policy differences. In return Scotland was required to provide seamen to serve in the English navy in times of warfare. Evidence for this can be found in the various Registers of the Privy Council of Scotland where levies were imposed on various ports to provide the seamen required to fulfill the Scottish government's commitment to the English Royal Navy, as shown in Volume III of the "Register of the Privy Council of Scotland" (3rd Series) covering 1672. Among the Exchequer Records at the Scottish Records Office is a collection entitled 'Navy Papers, 1615-1707' [SRO.E90], which include a receipt for 58 pressed men aboard HMS Colchester by order of the Lord Lyon, 23 March 1664, [SRO.E90/2] and a warrant for 300 seamen to be sent to London for service with the Royal Navy, 16 September 1664, with a list of names dated 1664/1665, [SRO.E90/3]. There are, however, relatively few documents extant which relate to the Scots Navy of the seventeenth century. A number of those which have survived have been included in James Grant's *"The Old Scots Navy, 1689-1710"*. Other information pertaining to this can be gleaned from various published volumes of the *"Register of the Privy Council of Scotland"* of the period. In 1707 the Union of Scotland and England resulted in a complete integration of Scotland's remaining, albeit minimal, naval forces within the Royal Navy.

Royal Naval records contain data on Scottish sailors from the mid-seventeenth century onwards. These records now reside mainly in the Public Record Office in London, but there remain some documents of relevance in the Scottish Records Office. Of these, the Clerk of Penicuik manuscripts [GD18] contain letters from Scots serving in the Royal Navy during the eighteenth century, and the Melville Castle papers [GD51] include significant material pertaining to the Royal Navy of the late eighteenth and early nineteenth centuries. The Bught Manuscripts [SRO.GD23.6.495] contain orders from the Admiralty in 1812 to gather men for the navy from the fishermen along the Moray Firth.

SCOTTISH MARITIME RECORDS

Letters of George Langlands, a cabin boy from Craichie in Angus [SRO.NRAS.0244/166-299] impressed into the Royal Navy in 1778, have recently been used in an article in the **Mariner's Mirror** entitled *"The Mercer Affair"* describing an incident between a Royal Navy vessel and an American privateer in 1777. Similarly, letters dated 1805 written by Midshipman Colin Campbell were the basis of D.B.Smith's article *"The Defiance at Trafalgar"* in the **Scottish Historical Review**, Volume XX.

The correspondence of a number of individual seafarers have found their way into various local archives. Letters of Archibald Buchanan who served as a midshipman at Spithead from 1803 to 1806 are in the **Glasgow City Archives**. Those of naval officer Alexander Falconer of Stonehaven, dated between 1810 and 1818 are in the **Moray Record Office**, and the letters 1735-1739 of Andrew Stivens, Lieutenant on HMS Lennox and later on HMS Louisa to his brother-in-law William Mowat in Stonehaven are in **Dundee University Archives** [DUA.BR.MS3.DC78]. Church Records, particularly the registers of baptism and marriages, include the occasional reference to naval personnel, and sometimes other sources such as a "list of communicants 1796 -1810" of the parish of Dundee [SRO.CH2.1218.57] include the names of sailors, their ships, and the names of wives, mothers or other relatives who drew part of their wages.

Individuals who served in the Royal Navy can also, to some extent, be identified from documentary evidence such as the published indexes to the probate records of the Prerogative Court of Canterbury. Among these are details of John Hogg from Dunbar, a mariner who died on HMS Falkland, probate 1698, and James Ferrier from Arbroath, a mariner who died on HMS Vanguard, probate 1694. Information can also be gleaned from the published indexes to the various Registers of Testaments within the Scottish Commissariat records. For example, Robert Speir from Irvine, a sailor on HMS Enterprise, cnf 1730 Commissariat of Glasgow, and Alexander MacKenzie, from St Andrews, a sailor on HMS Fury, cnf 1785 Commissariat of St Andrews, and elsewhere the will of David Burd, mariner on HMS Terrible, 1734 [SRO.RH15.54.39].

Among the documents of the Laing Charters is the probate and letters of administration of the will of David Knox, late of Edinburgh, Captain in the Royal Navy, dated 1795 by the Prerogative Court of Canterbury [Laing, #3282]. **The Laing Charters** also include the Commission by the Admiralty appointing Lieutenant John Fairbairn as Lieutenant of H.M. sloop The Speedy, dated 1803 [Laing, #3288].

Sometimes men who volunteered for, or were impressed into, a burgh's levy for the Royal Navy, were admitted on their return from service as burgesses

SCOTTISH MARITIME RECORDS

of their places of origin or residence. This applied only in communities such as Royal Burghs which had a degree of autonomy. Being a burgess brought many advantages, with a few obligations, and it was a much sought after position.

The *"Lockit Buik of Burgesses of Dundee, 1513-1981"* shows, "James Knight, skipper, for giving out for the town as a seaman to the King's service, 13 February 1715".

Two examples from the **Roll of Edinburgh Burgesses** are:

"Sir John Lindsay, Royal Navy, admitted as a burgess and guildsbrother of Edinburgh, gratis, by act of Council for good services, 22 October 1766", and:

"Captain John MacPherson in Philadelphia, Pennsylvania, late Commander of His Majesty's man o' war Britannia in the West Indies, by right of his father ... MacPherson, for good services, by Act of Council, 15.8.1764."

Newspapers are often overlooked by family historians, but they represent a treasure chest of genealogical data. Many of these are, however, inaccessible to the average researcher unless they can visit sources such as the **National Library of Scotland.** Among the many publications of A.J.Campbell is his *"Fife Deaths, 1822-1854",* based on contemporary Fife newspapers. This source is organised by towns and villages and then in alphabetical order of surnames, and is a unique and invaluable source for researchers. It includes a number of Fifers who had served in the Royal Navy, for example:

"Alexander Renny, mariner, a native of Inverkeithing, who was impressed in his early life and took part in Earl Howe's victory of 1 June 1794 stationed in the rigging of the Royal Sovereign, died at Low Lights, North Shields, 18 April 1843, aged 72".

[Source: The Fife Herald, 4 May 1843.]

The Scotsman carried a column entitled *"Naval Intelligence"* which provided information on various aspects of seafaring including promotions and appointments in the Royal Navy and the Coastguards. Similar columns can be found in other Scottish newspapers and in the **Scots Magazine.**

SCOTTISH MARITIME RECORDS

Select Bibliography

"The Admiral of Scotland", A.R.G.McMillan, in The Scottish Historical Review, Vol.XX, [Glasgow, 1923]
"In Defence of the Scottish Maritime Interest, 1681-1713", E.J.Graham, in The Scottish Historical Review, LXXI, [Edinburgh, 1992]
"James Ramsay, 1733-1789, Naval Surgeon & Naval Chaplain", Sir James Watt, in The Mariner's Mirror, Vol.81/2, [Greenwich, 1995]
"The Old Scots Navy, 1689-1710", J. Grant, [London, 1914]
"The Registers of the Privy Council of Scotland....." (series)
"Scottish Record Office, Source List No.9, Naval and Mercantile"
"The Vice Admiral of Scotland", Sir B. Seton, in The Scottish Historical Review, Vol.XX, [Glasgow, 1923]

SCOTTISH MARITIME RECORDS

MERCHANT NAVY

For centuries the monopoly of foreign trade was in the hands of the Royal Burghs and their ports. Only these could engage in international commerce and subsequently much of the coastal trade. During the seventeenth century the traditional trading links with ports on the Baltic, the North Sea, Scandinavia, France and Iberia were in the main from the east coast ports of Leith, Dundee and Aberdeen, while ports on the west coast such as Glasgow, Ayr and Dumfries dealt with western England, Ireland and the Biscayan ports. The rise of transatlantic commerce and the political union of Scotland and England in 1707 led to a rapid expansion of the Clyde ports of Greenock and Glasgow with the comparative decline of ports on the North Sea coast. The most prominent ports prior to the Industrial Revolution were Dunbar, Leith, Bo'ness, Kirkcaldy, Burntisland, Anstruther, Dundee, Montrose, Aberdeen, Inverness, Stromness, Greenock, Glasgow and Ayr.

Every port of any consequence had a mariners or seamen's society operating for the collective benefit of its members. Leading members of the seafaring communities, generally the skippers, set up controlling councils. Probably the most significant of their records as far as genealogists are concerned, are the contents of the Sea Boxes maintained by these societies. Before the start of a voyage each crew member subscribed to a fund, out of which their dependants would receive a pension in the event of his being lost at sea, or it would provide for support during illness or old-age. The voyages and the vessels of individual members can often be traced through the records of the Sea Box. Many of papers of these Sea Boxes have survived, but as they are all in their original manuscript form they require patient transcription by the reader. Some have been deposited with libraries or archives for safe-keeping. The **Sea Box of Bo'ness** is now with the **National Library of Scotland**, [NLS.Dep.259/60], that of Kirkcaldy is in the local museum, and **Perth & Kinross Archive** holds records of the **Perth Merchant Seamen's Fund 1824-1852** [B59.22.37-59].

James T. Davidson provides a useful insight into the contents and operation of a seamen's society in his *"The Prime Gilt Box of Kirkcaldy"*. The seamen's society in Kirkcaldy dates from the late sixteenth century although the surviving manuscript records commence in 1612. Davidson's work is based on the period 1612 to 1674 and covers topics such as the meaning of primegilt; the origins of the society, its lands and heritages; the dangers of piracy; prisoners of war; voyages; shipwrecked sailors; burials; and others.

SCOTTISH MARITIME RECORDS

The **Records of Trinity House, Leith**, kept in the SRO [GD.226] are a particularly useful source for genealogists. Among the contents are Minute Books, 1654-1912; financial records 1655-1958; letter books 1800-1941; pilotage records 1797-1922; and many more, (see 'The Port of Leith').

The cash book of Trinity House for the period 1712-1720 [SRO.GD26.12.25] shows payments to named poor seamen and their dependants, and the records of the **Free Fishermen of Newhaven** [SRO.GD265] date from 1572 and contain much material pertaining to this port. The SRO also holds the **Dysart Sailors Benefit Society 1836** [FS1.11.13]; **Sea Box of St Monance 1834** [FS1.11.28]; **Newburgh Shipmasters Friendly Society 1799** [FS1.1.35]; the **Friendly Society of Fishermen in Fisherrow 1821** [FS1.17.144]; **Society of Free Fishermen of Newhaven 1845** [FS1.17.171]; **Friendly Society of Shipmasters of Bo'ness 1757**; the Minute Book of the **Inverkeithing Sailors Society, 1835-1887** [B34.14]; and the **General Seabox of Bo'ness 1634** [FS1.26.6/7].

Documents which may throw light on the membership and activities of seamen's societies may be found in various official registers such as the **Register of Deeds**. Take for example the document registered under the name of John Ritchie, skipper in Fraserburgh, and treasurer of the Seabox of Fraserburgh, in 1700 [SRO.RD2.83.746]. This document is a bond for 200 merks subscribed to by John Hay, skipper in Fraserburgh, in favour of "Mr John Ritchie and Alexander Cuy, skippers there and present treasurers of the Seabox thereof, in Fraserburgh 7 December 1698, witnessed by Allan Bridge, James Middleton and Patrick Garden skippers there, and recorded in the Books of Council and Session on 10 January 1700". Burgh Records are another potential source of information on the lives of our seafaring ancestors. The **Inverkeithing Burgh Records** at the SRO contain, "an account given in to the Guildry of Inverkeithing by George Sime anent the Guildry's one-sixteenth part of his ship the Happy Janet of Inverkeithing which was wrecked on Portland beach" dated 28.5.1768 [SRO.B34.20.294].

The surviving records of the **Fraternity of Seamen, Trinity House, Dundee**, which have been deposited in **Dundee City Archives** contain examples of a range of documentation that could provide material of interest and relevance to the needs of the family historian. This material covers over three hundred years from the mid-seventeenth century to the present day. There are the Boxmasters Accounts 1652-1695, and a further five volumes covering the period 1824-1949; two volumes of cartularies 1766-1867; three volumes of sederunt books 1828-1916; pension lists 1851-1874; a typescript history of the Fraternity dated 1962; several volumes of admission books, Masters 1785-1861 and Mates

SCOTTISH MARITIME RECORDS

and Seamen 1799-1859; together with other material dating after 1850. The Index to Masters provides the date of admission to the Fraternity and the date of being made up as a Free Master. Examples are:

When admitted	Names	When made free
18 March 1816	Thomas Erskine	21 December 1819
17 December 1822	John A. Erskine	19 June 1827
21 March 1826	Thomas Ewing	15 March 1831
		[DCA.GD/Hu/SF/10/1]

As well as the seafarers own records there are sources within the public records which are of relevance. The Port Books of the seventeenth century, now in the Scottish Record Office [E71-E72], although incomplete, provide much useful data on ships, cargoes, skippers, merchants, and voyages. Sometimes they identify crew members who brought in goods subject to Customs duties. Dundee is fortunate in that there is an almost complete run of data pertaining to ships arriving there during the seventeenth century. This material is largely in its original manuscript form in a number of *"Registers of Shipping"* dating 1580-1589; 1612-1694; 1694-1700; and 1701-1713, to which must be added the published lists for the years 1580-1618 included in *"Wedderburn's Dundee Compt Book"*. A typical entry is:

"Dundee 27 November 1705 'the said day John Marr yr. master of the good ship the Helen of Dundie of burthen fourtie tunns, compeared and entered the same, come from Stockholm and loaded with iron & copper etc. In witness thereof he has submitted these present day and place foresaid. {signed} John Marr yr.'"

Other such shipping registers can be found elsewhere in Scotland. The **Glasgow City Archives** have those for the period 1763-1890 for Ayr, Campbelltown, Dumfries and Glasgow [Acc.3889]; Aberdeen 1824-1935 are in **Aberdeen City Archives**, and **Perth & Kinross Council Archive has Perth Registers of Shipping, 1824-1884,** [CE52.11.1-4].

Sometimes ship's logs and papers were deposited with local archives or libraries. **Dundee City Archives** have those of the brig Flora of Dundee for the period 1784-1790, and the account book of the brigantine Tagus of Dundee, 1796-1799. Among the **Ardgowan Estate Papers** [SRO.NRAS.1847] is the logbook of the brig Paddy Carey covering voyages from Greenock to New Orleans, Demerara, Brazil, and St Johns, New Brunswick, between 1825-1828. The SRO holds a microfilm of the personal record of John Dow, a sailor in Saltcoats, which describes trading voyages across the Atlantic from the Clyde to

SCOTTISH MARITIME RECORDS

North America and from Virginia to the West Indies, [RH4.43.1]; and Edward Burd's trading voyage from Leith to Newfoundland and Barcelona in 1726-1727 is contained in his journal [RH9.14.102]. **Dundee University Archives** hold the papers of Robert Ferrier, a shipmaster in Dundee, which include the inventory of the sloop Isabella, ca.1770, [DUA.MS57.3.1] and those of John P. Ingram, former Shipping Correspondent of the *'Dundee Courier'* comprising 38 notebooks of a miscellany of information such as local shipbuilders, crew members, and vessels 1767-1980, [DUA.MS73].

The records of Customs and Excise of the eighteenth century, as a source for family historians, have been dealt with by Frances Wilkins in her classic works *"Scottish Customs and Excise Records ... from 1707 onwards"* and *"Family Histories in Scottish Customs Records"*. The former book contains a concise history of the Customs and Excise in Scotland, identifying the types of records available and their present locations. It also provides insight into the Letter Books, and gives examples of material and information to be found, particularly in the **Greenock Customs House.** Bureaucratic necessity required local authorities to maintain records of income and expenditure relating to docks under their control, but sadly few of these have survived. Those of Aberdeen have been in part published under the title *"Aberdeen Shore Works 1596-1670"*, providing much useful information for the genealogist and local historian. Similar material, but in manuscript form, exists elsewhere, as with **Dundee City Archives** *"The Shoremasters Account Book of Dundee 1753 - 1800"*.

Indentures of Apprenticeships which include apprentice sailors, were important documents, often recorded within burgh registers of deeds. The SRO holds a number of these manuscripts. George Reid, son of the late William Reid, a merchant burgess of Edinburgh, is a listed mariner, as is Captain John Arnot, commander of the Jacob of Pittenweem, shown to be indentured for two years in 1706 [SRO.RH9.19.279]. Such documents can also be found in various burgh registers of deeds. The indenture of apprenticeship between John Auchenleck and Alexander Jarron is in the **Dundee Register of Deeds**, and the two page document begins:

"At Dundee 25 March 1752 it is agreed between John Auchenleck, shipmaster in Dundee, on the one part and Alexander Jarron, lawful son to the deceased David Jarron in Carmyllie with the consent of William Jarron, cowfeeder in Dundee, and James Husband, maltman there, his cautioners ... that Alexander Jarron becomes and binds himself apprentice and servant to and with the said John Auchenleck for learning of and serving him in the sailor's art or calling and that for the full space of five years from the date hereof...."

[Dundee City Archives: RD471.767].

SCOTTISH MARITIME RECORDS

Those with an interest in Fife may be familiar with the work of the aforementioned Andrew J. Campbell, who produced a number of excellent publications pertaining to that region. His *"Some Fife Apprentices, 1524-1897"*, Volume 2, contains abstracts of indentureship agreements found in various Burgh Court Records, Fife Sheriff Court Records, and the Books of Council and Session. Again, these contain also of a number of young men apprenticed as sailors:

"Charles Wilson, Inverkeithing, son of Charles Wilson, carpenter 'presently abroad' was apprenticed to William Walker, tenant in Orchardhead, and John Walker in Inverkeithing, owners of the sloop *The Six Sisters of Inverkeithing* in the navigation and seafaring business for 3 years from 17 March 1812."

[SRO.B34.8.1.pp15-16]

Apprenticeship in the local burgh, under an existing burgess, merchant or craftsman, was one method of being admitted to that most coveted position, a burgess. Recorded in the manuscript *"Lockit Buik of Burgesses of Dundee 1513-1981"*, is one Robert Mawer, a former apprentice of James Raitt, shipmaster and burgess of Dundee, who on 25 April 1733 was admitted as a burgess by this method. Occasionally a town council would grant the title of burgess to someone who had performed exceptional service to the community. Among the honorary burgesses and guildbrethren of Glasgow was one Humphrey Cunningham, a ship mate in Port Glasgow, admitted on 23 May 1773, due to his *"spirited behaviour in quelling the late mobs at Greenock and at Port Glasgow"*.

The **James Watt Memorial Library in Greenock** holds an index to births, marriages and deaths of Scots abroad, taken from local newspapers between 1802-1914, and includes a number of seafarers. From the late eighteenth century onwards newspapers supplied information on shipping movements, and this can be a useful tool with which to track ships and their company. Correspondents recorded other aspects of seafaring from smuggling to shipwrecks. The **Aberdeen Journal**, a newspaper which dates from 1747, regularly carried information on shipping, particularly vessels belonging to the northeast. In issue number 4747, dated 2 January 1839, it has arrivals and departures reports from Aberdeen, Thurso, Banff, Peterhead, Fraserburgh and Stromness. The **Scotsman's** *"Naval Intelligence"* column of Wednesday, 2 January 1850 is divided into geographical regions and includes *"East India shipping"*, movements of ships to and from the Indian sub continent; *"Sound Intelligence"* reports on vessels entering or leaving the Baltic via the Sound

SCOTTISH MARITIME RECORDS

between Denmark and Sweden; *"Leith Shipping"*, arrivals at this port, and the *"Glasgow Shipping List"*, information on vessels registered in the Clyde.

Select Bibliography

"Aberdeen Shore Works Accounts, 1596-1670", L.B.Taylor, [Aberdeen, 1972]
"Account of what most remarkable happened to us on our voyage from Dundee in
    Scotland to New Edinburgh in New Caledonia, ...1700." in The Darien
    Papers, 1695-1700, [Edinburgh, 1849]
"The Compt Buik of David Wedderburn, merchant in Dundee, 1587-1630",
    plus 'Shipping Lists of Dundee, 1580-1618', A.H.Miller, [Edinburgh, 1898]
"The Foreign Trade of Dumfries and Kirkcudbright, 1672-1696", T.C.Smout,
    in Transactions of the Dumfries and Galloway NHA, (3rd), Vol.XXXVII,
    [Dumfries, 1960]
"The History of Inverkeithing and Rosyth", W.Stephen, [Aberdeen, 1921]
"History of Port Glasgow", J.MacArthur, [Glasgow, 1932]
"Instructions and Sailing orders to the Commander of the ship Margaret",
    in The Darien Papers, 1695-1700, [Edinburgh, 1849]
"Journals of the Voyage of the ship Margaret," in The Darien Papers, 1695-1700,
    [Edinburgh, 1849]
"Letters from Dumfries to a Scottish Factor at Rotterdam 1676-1683",
    T.C.Smout, in Transactions of the Dumfries and Galloway NHA, (3rd),
    Vol.XXXVIII, [Dumfries, 1963]
"The Overseas Trade of Ayrshire, 1660-1707", T.C.Smout, in Ayrshire
    Collections, No.6, [Ayr, 1961]
"The Port of Aberdeen", V.E.Clark, [Aberdeen, 1921]
"The Port of Leith", S.Mowat, [Edinburgh, 1994]
"The Port of Montrose", D.Adam, [Montrose, 1993]
"The Prime Gilt Box of Kirkcaldy", James T. Davidson, [Kirkcaldy, 1946]
"Sailing Instructions to Captain William Tennant, 20 August 1697." in
    The Darien Papers, 1695-1700, [Edinburgh, 1849]
"Scotland and the Atlantic. The voyage of the Jonet of Leith, December 1611."
    R.U.Hunter, in Mariner's Mirror Vol.79/1, [Greenwich, 1993]
"Scotland's North Sea Gateway - Aberdeen Harbour 1136-1986", J.Turner,
    [Aberdeen, 1986]
"Scottish Customs & Excise Records with particular reference to Strathclyde
    from 1707 onwards.", F. Wilkins, [Blakedown, 1992]
"Scottish Shipping, 1775-1805", G. Jackson, in Shipping, Trade and Commerce,
    editors P.L.Cottrell & D.H.Aldcroft, [Leicester, 1981]
"The Scottish Staple at Veere", J.Davidson and A.Gray, [London, 1909]

SCOTTISH MARITIME RECORDS

"Scottish Trade with Sweden 1580-1622", J.Dow, in Scottish Historical Review, Vol.XLVIII, [Aberdeen, 1969]

"Shipwrecks of North East Scotland, 1444-1990", D.M.Ferguson, [Aberdeen, 1991]

"A Short History of the Shipmaster Society or The Seaman's Box in Aberdeen" A.Clark, [Aberdeen, 1911]

"Skipper from Leith", W.S.Terry, [Philadelphia, 1962]

"The Trade and Shipping of Dundee, 1780-1850", G.Jackson, [Dundee, 1990]

SCOTTISH MARITIME RECORDS

FISHING

During the seventeenth century the Dutch were, without doubt, the leading maritime power in Europe. The seafaring supremacy of the Dutch was based on their fishing tradition; in 1620 the Dutch were thought to have had nearly 2000 fishing vessels operating in the North Sea alone. Their pre-eminence was maintained through technological innovations such as the drift net and the "herring buss", a boat designed especially for fishing.

In order to protect and nourish the British domestic fishing fleets, laws were passed which virtually prohibited the Dutch from fishing off the coasts of Scotland and England, and later banished them from British ports. The Anglo-Dutch wars of the seventeenth century also contributed to the decline of Dutch supremacy in the North Sea fishing grounds. During this century also, the government encouraged the development of the herring fishery by establishing the Royal Fishing Company in 1677. The selection of Greenock as the Company's main base of operations caused an expansion of the infrastructure, and a corresponding expansion in the pool of skilled and experienced seamen there. Records of the **Society of Free Fishermen of Newhaven** [SRO.GD265] 1572-1935, probably represent the largest collection of its kind. To be found among this material are manuscripts of correspondence 1797-1909, property writs and related papers 1572-1885, petitions 1700 and 1803-1885, miscellaneous legal papers 1624-1909, and accounts 1830-1888. There are also volumes of accounts 1816-1890, funeral books 1820-1886, rent ledgers 1829-1889, sick benefit payments 1832-1889, and minute books 1805-1876. One of the early manuscripts is a Letter of Lawburrows dated 30 May 1625:

"raised at the instance of Robert Or, fisher, indweller in Newheavin, Helen Wilsoun his spouse, and Thomas Robesoun his son-in-law, against Norman Hunter, fisher, indweller in Newheavin, Isabel Wallis his spouse, Gilbert Hunter his brother, and Thomas Glassfurd, servant to the said Norman."
[SRO.GD265.4.1.3].

The SRO also holds a document listing skippers from ports throughout south-east Scotland and fishing off Dunbar in 1706, [SRO.GD26.15.21].

Family and estate papers sometimes contain references to seafaring, for example the Leven and Melville Muniments have a list of children from Crail whose fishermen fathers had been drowned at sea in 1768. This list gives the children's names, ages, and amounts received [SRO.GD26.12.25].

SCOTTISH MARITIME RECORDS

From the mid-eighteenth century on, the government again began to provide support for the fishing industry, especially herring fishing, and between 1752-1796 the paid bounties to encourage its growth. From the surviving records, now in the SRO [E508/49/9-96/9], it is possible to identify skippers, their crews and vessels. Some of these documents are particularly detailed; the record of the bounty paid at Campbeltown in 1775 to the Sally of Rothesay, whose skipper was named John McKirdy, lists the ship's eleven crew members, together with their ages and physical description [SRO.E508.74.9.405]

The foundation of the **British Fisheries Society** in 1785 led to significant developments in the infrastructure of the fishing industry, including the construction and renovation of harbours and "fishertouns". Examples of these works are the towns of Ullapool in Wester Ross, and Pultneytown, by Wick. The SRO holds papers of the British Fishery Society [GD9] which contains useful genealogical data. The **Tobermory Pier Duties, 1831-1836** [GD9.68] lists vessels, masters and cargoes.

In 1808 an Act "for the further encouragement and better regulation" of the Scots herring industry was passed, impacting significantly on the structure and operation of the fishing industry. Records of the Fishery Board, set up to administer the industry, dated 1809-1939 can be found among the **Department of Agriculture and Fisheries Papers** in the SRO [AF.1.38]. Within these papers are letters such as the one dated 1836 on behalf of Donald McGrigor, fisherman on the Isle of Tanera, for money to be shared with Robert McLeod for the purpose of building a new boat; "they are both very poor men, each having a wife and eight children to support" [SRO.AF35.6.2]. The published **Annual Reports of the Commissioners for the Herring Industry** date from 1815, and contain statistics, illustrations of harbour plans and specifications, and lists of fishermen. The lists are entitled "Allowances to Poor Fishermen for repairing their boats" and are analysed by district, names of fishermen, places of residence, and the sums allowed. The Annual Report of 1831 reads:

"The Allowances to Poor Fishermen" gives the undernoted for the District of Anstruther:

George Ramsay	Crail	£2.00.00
Robert Muir	Cellardyke	£4.10.00
John Gowns	St Monance	£3.00.00
John Hutt	St Monance	£3.00.00
George Smith, sr.	Cellardyke	£5.00.00

paid over by George Smith, officer at Anstruther"

SCOTTISH MARITIME RECORDS

Local libraries often contain unique source material. The **Scottish Fisheries Museum Library** has a three volume typescript work entitled *"Anecdotes of Fish and Fishermen in the East Neuk of Fife, 1452-1955"*, written and compiled by William Martin in 1977. Newspapers also should not be overlooked as a useful source of genealogical data. The "Pittenweem Register" of 15 and 22 May 1846 reports that "John Oliphant, from St Monance, member of the crew of the sloop Altnaskeach of Pittenweem, was drowned 12 May 1847 in consequence of a shipwreck on the banks of the Tay". Sir John Sinclair's *"Old Statistical Accounts of Scotland, 1791-1799"* contains useful local information on fishing and seafaring in general.

Select Bibliography

"Auld Buckhyne" F. Rankin [Wemyss, 1986]
"Bluecoats, Skate-mooed Pooches and Strippet Brots: Auchmithie and Arbroath Fisher dress" in The Costume Society of Scotland: Bulletin No.XXXIII [Edinburgh, 1993]
"Book of Buchan" A.Tocher, [Peterhead, 1910]
"The British Fisheries Society, 1786-1893" J. Dunlop, [Edinburgh, 1978]
"Fisheries in North East Scotland before 1800", J.R.Coull, in Scottish Studies, Vol.13, [Edinburgh, 1969]
"Fishing and Whaling", A. Martin, [Edinburgh, 1995]
"Fishing Boats and Fisher Folk on the East Coast of Scotland", P. Anson [London, 1930]
"The Fishing Industries of Scotland, 1790-1914", M.Gray, [Oxford, 1978]
"Focus on Fishing - Arbroath and Gourdon", E.Hay and B.Walker, [Dundee, 1985]
"Fraserburgh, Past and Present", J.Cranna, [Aberdeen, 1914]
"History of the Society of Free Fishermen of Newhaven", R.M.Black, [Edinburgh, 1951]
"Kilrenny and Cellardyke", H.D.Watson, [Edinburgh, 1986]
"The Lammas Drave and the Winter Herrin'", P. Smith, [Edinburgh, 1985]
"Marriage and Traditions in Fishing Communities", M.H.King, in Review of Scottish Culture, No.8, [Edinburgh, 1993]
"Newhaven on Forth, Port of Grace" T. McGowran [Edinburgh, 1985]
"An Old Time Fishing Town - Eyemouth", D. McIver, [Greenock, 1906]
"Scottish Sail - a forgotten era", R.Simper, [Newton Abbot, 1974]
"Sea Fisheries of Scotland", J.R.Coull, [Edinburgh, 1996]
"Shetland Fishing Saga" C.A.Goodlad, [Lerwick, 1971]
"Shetland Life and Trade" H. Smith, [Edinburgh, 1984]
"Tradition and Innovation in the life of a fisherman's wife on the Buchan coast", G.Munro, in Review of Scottish Culture, No.8, [Edinburgh, 1993]

SCOTTISH MARITIME RECORDS

WHALING

For nearly 200 years Scotland played a relatively significant role in the whaling industry. Whaling, as a commercial enterprise, seems to have been developed initially by the Basques but by the seventeenth century it was dominated by the Dutch. During the seventeenth century began a Scottish involvement in whaling, albeit in a small way. Some boats operated directly from Scotland, while a number of Scots seamen were employed on Dutch and English vessels. There was, for example, at least one Scot on Barentz's voyage to the Arctic in 1595. The earliest Scottish mariner known to have sailed to Greenland was a John Cunningham aboard his ship The Lion via the Cumberland Sound to the coast of Labrador in 1606. Whaling grounds of this period were off Spitzbergen, Iceland and the east coast of Greenland.

Scotland's first attempt to establish a whaling industry occurred in 1617, when James VI granted a patent to the Scottish East India and Greenland Company, to fish off the coast of Greenland. The company did operate off the coast of Spitzbergen and sent at least one cargo of "trayne oyle" back to Leith, before its activities had to be suspended because of conflict with the English Muscovy Company which felt that its monopoly was endangered. In 1626 Charles I granted Nathaniel Udward a warrant to trade and fish in Greenland for oil which he required for his Leith soapworks. Edward, however, subcontracted to whaling crews based in Yarmouth, which in turn led to rivalry with whaling crews of the English Muscovy Company in Spitzbergen during 1632, and again the Scottish operation was suspended. There was yet another attempt to develop an indigeneous Scots whaling industry in 1670 when Charles II granted a 19-year monopoly of trade with Greenland, Iceland, etc to the Scots Fishing Company. Overall, the level of Scottish participation before the mid-eighteenth century could best be described as peripheral to the activities of the Dutch, and increasingly the English.

From the mid-eighteenth century onwards, however, Scotland became increasingly prominent as a whaling nation. In 1733 the British Government, keen to encourage the expansion of the fishing industry and to increase its maritime power, began to offer bounties of £1 per ton of shipping to British based vessels engaged in whaling. This did persuade some English ships to enter the industry but it was not until 1749, when the bounty was doubled, that Scottish firms and many additional English companies began to participate. Among the early Scots firms to enter the industry were the Edinburgh Whale Fishing Company in 1750, the Aberdeen Whale Fishing Company in 1752, and the Dundee Whale Fishing Company in 1754. According to a Parliamentary report there were 367 whaling voyages from Scotland between 1750 and 1786, from the

SCOTTISH MARITIME RECORDS

ports of Leith, Greenock, Campbelltown, Bo'ness, Dunbar, Port Glasgow, Aberdeen, Kirkcaldy, Anstruther, Montrose, and shortly afterwards from Peterhead. In the main these were to the whaling grounds off Greenland, and latterly to the Davis Strait.

The crews of Scottish whaling ships had more than the natural perils encountered during voyages at sea to deal with. They had to reckon with both the King's enemies (the Americans during the American War of Independence and the French during the Napoleonic Wars), and the Royal Navy, or more specifically the Press Gang. Bounty records, which provide complete crew lists, reveal that it was not uncommon for the ordinary seamen to abandon ship off the Scottish coast to avoid a Press gang known to be lying in ambush. Frequently whaling ships would arrive back at their home ports with skeleton crews comprised of the skipper, the harpooners, the line managers, and the apprentices; all the seamen having gone ashore earlier. Half of the crew of the Advice of Dundee, master James Webster, went ashore near Duncansby Head on 31 July 1806 on the voyage home to Dundee from the Davis Strait. [SRO.E508.107.8]

Information concerning the industry during the seventeenth century is minimal and much of what exists is in the **Scottish Record Office** among the Clerk of Penicuik papers [GD18] and the Merchant Company of Edinburgh papers [GD277]. From the mid-eighteenth century onwards, however, there is significant documentary material in the SRO particularly the Bounty Records [SRO.E508/47/8 to 130/8] which identify, among other things, the vessels, their crews and voyages. Contemporary newspapers such as the **Aberdeen Journal** note the departure and return of whaling ships and record their cargoes. They also contain reports of successes or failures based on information brought back by other whaling vessels. The **Edinburgh Evening Courant** No.18746, dated Thursday 5 January 1832 has an article describing the 'wintering of the boat's crew of the John of Greenock at Operniwick, Baffin's Bay'. The SRO has a miscellany of source material such as the log book of the St Anns from Aberdeen to Greenland and return, including instructions on whaling, 1756, [SRO.GD345.1241] and papers concerning the Aberdeen and the Edinburgh Whale Fishing Companies, 1750-1771, [SRO.GD345.763]. **Dundee University** has the papers of two local whaling companies, the Dorothy Whale Fishing Company and the Friendship Whale Fishing Company, dated 1829-1837, [DUA.MS57.3.2/5] and substantial material regarding the Tay Whaling Company dating from 1791, including details of voyages, ships, catches, skippers and crews.

SCOTTISH MARITIME RECORDS

Select Bibliography

"Fishing and Whaling", A.Martin, [Edinburgh, 1995]
"A Narrative of the Sufferings of the Crew of the Dee in 1836", G.Clark, [Aberdeen, 1837]
"Peterhead's Whaling Years", G. Sutherland, in Scottish Local History, Vol.30 [Edinburgh, 1994]
"The Peterhead Whaling Trade", A. Buchan, [Peterhead, 1993]
"The Ransoming of Eliza Shaw", D.A. Petrie
The Sufferings of the Ice Bound Whalers", J.Bain, [Edinburgh, 1836]
"The Whale Hunters", R. Smith, [Edinburgh, 1993]
"The Whaling Years, Peterhead 1788-1893", G. Sutherland, [Aberdeen, 1993]
"Whales and whaling", A.G.Credland, [Aylesbury, 1982]

SCOTTISH MARITIME RECORDS

SMUGGLING

Smuggling was a long established practice among seafarers along the coasts of Scotland. Scottish smugglers were active also in America, before 1707, circumventing the English Navigation Acts which in practice banned any non-English vessel from trading there. The imposition of the English Customs and Excise system in 1707 led to the rapid expansion of smuggling, particularly off the east coast of Scotland. All levels of society seem to have engaged directly and indirectly in smuggling goods, and the practice was not limited to seafarers. Although, as one might expect, the smugglers themselves did not keep records, there are many references to smuggling and smugglers in the records of the Customs and Excise. Most of these have survived, and are partly held in appropriate archives depending on the precinct involved, and partly in the Scottish Record Office. In recent years significant research has been done into these records, resulting in a number of publications which are highly appropriate to the needs of the family historian.

Select Bibliography

"The Customs Accounts of Dumfries and Kirkcudbright, 1560-1660", A.Murray, in Transactions of the Dumfries and Galloway NHA, (3rd), Vol.XLII, [1966]
"Customshouse letters to the Officers at Dunbar, 1765", T.C.Smout, in East Lothian Antiquarian & Field Naturalists Society, Vol.XI, [1968]
"Dumfries & Galloway's Smuggling Story", F. Wilkins, [Blakedown, 1993]
"Eighteenth century Scottish Smugglers: the evidence from Montrose and Dumfries", R. Goring, in Review of Scottish Culture, Vol.3, [Edinburgh, 1987]
"Family Histories in Scottish Customs Records", F.Wilkins, [Blakedown, 1993]
"The King's Customs Administration in Aberdeen, 1750-1815", T. Donnelly, in Northern Scotland, Vol.16, [Aberdeen, 1996]
"The Maltmen, Customs and Excisemen of Dundee, 1700-1850", A.Pellow, [Dundee, 1991]
"Selections from the Customs Records Preserved at Dumfries", B.R.Leftwich, in Transactions of the Dumfries and Galloway N.H.A., (3rd), Vol.XVII, 1931
"The Smuggling Story of the Northern Shores", F.Wilkins, [Blakedown, 1995]
"The Smuggling Story of Two Firths", F.Wilkins, [Blakedown, 1993]
"The Smugglers", D. Fraser, [Montrose, 1978]
"Smuggling in Eighteenth century Orkney", W.S.Hewison, in Orkney Misc No.3
"Smuggling in the North Channel in the Eighteenth Century", L.M.Cullen, in Scottish Economic Social and Economic History, Vol 7, [Edinburgh, 1987]
"Strathclyde's Smuggling Story", F.Wilkins, [Blakedown, 1992]

SCOTTISH MARITIME RECORDS

PRIVATEERS AND PIRATES

During periods of warfare many shipowners took to privateering, an arrangement whereby the government authorised armed merchant ships (privateers) to attack and seize enemy shipping. Privateering became a lucrative business, built up by seizing 'prizes' at sea. Many considered it legalised piracy. Perhaps the most famous, or infamous Scottish privateer was William Kidd. Kidd had been born in Dundee, the son of a local seaman, and after a period of time spent in Greenock, settled in New York as a shipmaster. During the 1690s he was the skipper of a New York based privateer, but eventually turned to outright piracy, leading to his execution by drowning, at Wapping in 1703. Captain Kidd was not the only Scot who engaged in piracy or privateering, though Scottish records are more likely to contain descriptions of privateering than piracy, unless Scots vessels were the victims. Take for example:-

"2 July 1593. John Simson, clerk of the Susanna of Aberdeen, 150 tons, John Stirling in Torry, mariner, Thomas Mill, mariner in Torry, Alexander Knollis, burgess of Aberdeen, and John Gardner, mariner, stated that the said ship left the Port of Fittie, Aberdeen, on 6 July 1588, laden with salmond for Dieppe. They remained there for 20 days and went to Bordeaux and there were freighted by Gascon merchants, resident in Bordeaux, to Middelburg in Flanders, there they were freighted by Middelburg merchants for a voyage to Spain laden with "pakine and pype ballis and cofferis of merchandis such as silk, holland cloth, cambric, extending to 50 packs". At St Lukar de Baremeda a ship from Rusio in Brittany called the Janet, master and skipper Christia Pappa, accused John Murray, master and skipper of the Susanna and his crew of piracy and theft which led to their imprisonment. Subsequently at a trial they were found not guilty but then Christian Pappa accused them of being Protestants and Lutherans which led to their apprehension, some were burnt, others committed to the gallows, some into slavery, others died in prison, while the ship and its cargo, worth 60,000 ducats, were impounded."

Source: Aberdeen Burgh Records, Testimonial Book, in Miscellany of the Spalding Club, II, [Aberdeen, 1940]

As privateering was state authorised there exist records of the licences or "Letters of Marque" issued by the government authorising skippers to engage in privateering. Some of these are contained in the various **"Registers of the Privy Council of Scotland"**, including: Letters of Marque issued to William Forrester, master of the James of Dundee, and to Thomas Auchenleck, master of the Golden Lion of Dundee, 16.1.1627 [RPC.1.495/500] to Captain John Masterton, master of the Providence of Dundee, against the French, Danes and Dutch, 21.6.1666, by

SCOTTISH MARITIME RECORDS

the Privy Council. [RPC.3rd.2.642], and to Walter Rankine, master of the Christian of Dundee, 9.12.1626 [RPC.1.481/505].

When, on 4 May 1691 Ninian Gibson, described as a merchant of Glasgow, was issued with letters of marque and commissioned by the Privy Council of Scotland as captain of the Lamb of Glasgow, 100 tons burthen, with 20 pieces of ordnance he was instructed:

"to set forth and goe to sea and search for, follow and pursue after, as also to take, seize upon, and apprehend and in the case of resistance to fyre, sink or destroy the shipps and goods of the French, Irish or Scottish highlands in rebellion.."

[Register of the Privy Council of Scotland, XVI.277]

Information on privateering can also be found in unlikely places. The following is quoted from the Acts of the Parliaments of Scotland:

"The Estaits of Parliament .....doe heirby thairfoir authorize with full power and comissioun Captaine Johne Gillespie, Captain of ye schip callit the Elizabeth of Kirkcaldie to protect secur and defend all the merchand schips of the kingdome in the exereing of thair lawful trade from the violence and wrongs of the Irish frigotts and piratts ..." 1649.

[Vol.VI, Part II, fo.494]

The SRO also holds Letters of Marque including that issued to John Wemyss, master of the privateer Wemyss of Burntisland 1666. [SRO.GD29.43].

The SRO holding includes documents concerning a number pertaining to privateering. The papers concerning the Providence of Valleyfield, captured by a French privateer and taken to Dunkirk in 1676 [SRO.GD29.1480-3] is one such, and the decree of the Admiralty Court concerning the Dutch ship taken by John Wemyss master of the privateer Wemyss of Burntisland 1666, [SRO.GD29.43] is another.

Dumfries & Galloway Archives contain a precept signed by John Copland to Andrew Bell, treasurer, dated 21 August 1703, to pay 40 shilling Scots to Mistress Douglas

"ane object of charity who wes taken by the French privateers in her passage from Dublin, wes spoild of her goods ... to help her on her way to Glasgow".

[DGA:RB2.2.17].

SCOTTISH MARITIME RECORDS

In April 1706 the St Andrew, master Charles Charters, laden with a cargo of wine and other commodities, was seized when sailing home to Leith by a privateer from Middleburg, where the cargo was subsequently sold. This was generally thought to be a reprisal for a German ship having been taken by Captain Gordon. [Source: Acts of Parliament, Volume XI, 1702-1707, appendix 122]. The Registers of the Privy Council of Scotland contain occasional reference to piracy. In July 1642 the Privy Council received a complaint from William Cobb that his fishing vessel The Roe had been seized by pirates off the island of Lewis. A claim which was denied by Oliver Mowat, a Stornaway merchant. [RPCS.VII]

For centuries, Moorish corsairs preyed on European merchant ships and later American vessels in the Mediterranean and the Atlantic. There are many references to these activities in Scottish records, especially in the form of Church appeals for contributions towards ransoms to gain the release of seamen and others held prisoner in the North African strongholds of these pirates. During the seventeenth century the Privy Council authorised church collections, and the published Registers are a good source providing often the name of the vessel, the names of captain and crew, ports of destination and origin, and the place and date of the ship's capture. One such report details that on 15 November 1677 the Privy Council received a petition from Robert Williamson, a Montrose skipper, master of the Isabel of Montrose, who with his ship and crew had been captured by a Turkish man o' war while sailing home from La Rochelle with a cargo of salt and brandy, and subsequently imprisoned in Tangiers. The names of the crew of the Isabel were David Wood, the mate, William Williamson, Thomas Hogg, David Simpson, William Drimmie, James Bonar, William Woods, James Butchart and John Millar, mariners.

The Town Council recommendation that a collection be made by the local churches towards the necessary ransom is outlined in the pages of Marguerite Wood's "**Extracts from the Records of the Burgh of Edinburgh, 1665-1680**" [Edinburgh, 1950], page 342. This, and similar volumes, are very useful for maritime references relating to Leith.

The **Aberdeen Journal** {#2230, 11 October 1790}, reported that in September 1790 The Peggy, whose master was Captain Marquis, arrived at Greenock from Leghorn, with Charles Colville, a native of Arbroath on board. Picked up in Algiers, Colville had been captured with Captain O'Bryen and 15 other crew members by an Algerian 'Xebec' in July 1785 from the brig The Dolphin of Philadelphia, and taken into slavery. Of the crew of this American ship, four were Scots; Charles Colville, John Robertson, son of John Robertson a

SCOTTISH MARITIME RECORDS

cooper in Glasgow, George Smith from Portsoy, and William Paterson from Aberdeen. Six of the crew died of plague in 1788. The more fortunate Colville was rescued by the payment of a £350 ransom, paid in part by his friends, and by partly by George Dempster of Dunnichen who had negotiated his release through Charles Logie, the British Consul in Algiers. Colville brought home letters from the less fortunate, remaining Scots prisoners.

The **Aberdeen Journal** carried a report on a piracy trial in Edinburgh at the late date of 1821. This concerned the Jane of Gibralter, Captain Thomas Johnson, who, with a crew including two Scots David Robertson Strachan and Peter Smith, sailed from Gibralter bound for Brazil in June 1820. Some of the crew mutinied and took over the ship, subsequently landing on Barra where they were apprehended by the local Customs officer.

A few years later a Fife vessel was attacked off South America. An extract from a letter by Captain James Hossack of The Henry to the owners in Kirkcaldy, from Beunos Ayres dated 23.11.1825 reads:

"*I was boarded upon the Equator in longitude 22 degrees 10 minutes West by a Columbian privateer mounting 14 guns, 75 men. He took provisions from me to the amount of $73 and sent to me on board $50 stating I was well paid. The vessel's name was the Romana, Captain Pablo Ortiz, belonging to La Guayra. In Latitude 10 degrees 23 minutes North and 67 degrees 15 minutes West lay some days before to his boarding The Henry he took a Spanish brig from the coast of Africa with 450 slaves on board and had them sail to the Havannah for sale.*"

[Fife Herald #204, 2.2.1826.]

Select Bibliography

"Jacobite Privateers in the Nine Year War.", J.S.Bromley, in Corsairs and
    Navies, 1660-1760, [London, 1987]
"The Mercer Affair", R.J.Adam, in The Mariner's Mirror Vol.80,
    [Greenwich, 1994]
"The Port of Aberdeen", V.E.Clark, [Aberdeen, 1921]
"Scots who were victims of fierce Turkish pirates", G. Johnson, in the Leopard,
    No.197, [Ellon, 1994]

SCOTTISH MARITIME RECORDS

THE SLAVE TRADE

It may be surprising learn that Scottish ships and seamen were engaged in the notorious Slave Trade, and were part of the Triangular Trade between Europe, Africa and America. Certainly, this business overwhelmingly was operated out of the ports of London, Bristol and Liverpool, but on a small scale also involved Glasgow and Montrose. There are known to have been trading voyages from Scotland to the Gulf of Guinea as early as the 1630s, but the Slave Trade seems to been small scale in the eighteenth century. Individual Scots are, however, known to have served aboard English ships engaged in slaving along the Guinea coast during the seventeenth century, as evidenced from their wills probated by the Prerogative Court of Canterbury.

In Horseburgh v. Bogle [SRO.AC9/1042], a case which came before the High Court of the Admiralty in 1728, Alexander Horseburgh, a surgeon in Glasgow, had been the supercargo aboard the Hanover of Glasgow, Captain Garrett, and was accused by his employers Robert Bogle jr., John Gray, Arthur Tran, and Samuel McCaull, merchants in Glasgow, of mishandling transactions during a voyage to Guinea and St Kitts in 1719. The process included Horseburgh's ledgers covering transactions along the coast of Guinea and in St Kitts alongside letters written during the voyage.

A case before the **Court of Session** in 1763 [SRO.CS96, invoice book no.502] reveals that Buchanan and Simpson, merchants in Glasgow, sent a ship to Angola and afterwards sold slaves in Jamaica. **Montrose Museum** has among its manuscript collection a charter party involving a slaving voyage from Montrose via Holland to West Africa, and from there to the West Indies and the Chesapeake before returning home.

The **Aberdeen Journal** (No 246) reported:

"Glasgow 18 September 1752. We have advice that one of the Montrose Guineamen is arrived in the Potomac River, Virginia, consigned to Mr William Black. The sale of Negro men at £32 and for women £30 sterling..."

Select Bibliography

"Montrose Slaving Ships", D. Dobson, in The Leopard, No197, [Ellon, 1994]

SCOTTISH MARITIME RECORDS

COURT RECORDS

Records of Courts of Law, both central and local, contain much of relevance to the family historian. For the period under consideration there are three distinct central courts: the Court of Session (the supreme civil court), the Admiralty Court, and the High Court of the Justiciary (the supreme criminal court). Admiralty Court is the most relevant to this purpose, and its records residing in the SRO, date from 1557 to 1830, after which date the main judicial functions were transferred to the Court of Session.

The High Court of the Admiralty of Scotland

The records of this institution, which are now kept in West Register House, Edinburgh, contain a substantial amount of material of interest. They date to 1830, after which many of the responsibilities of the court were transferred to London. Because of the vagueness of indexing of the material, together with its copiousness, the use of these manuscripts is a daunting task which very few scholars, let alone genealogists, are willing to undertake. However, it is the case that these voluminous records are currently being analysed with the objective of providing a "Guide to the Admiralty Records". Those interested in this source should read Sue Mowat's article on what is in the records and how to access them, in **Scottish Local History** Volume 36, [Edinburgh, 1996].

Sample abstracts from the Admiralty Court Records:-

"William Porter and John Niven, late sailors on the Agnes and Jean of Ayr, and Zacharias Gemmell, their factor, against William Reid, shipmaster in Ayr, for wages due on the following voyage, lasting from April 9, 1730, to October 6, 1731; Clyde to Hamburg, thence to Cork in Ireland, thence to the Madeiras, thence to Barbados, thence to Virginia thence to Antigua, thence to Port Glasgow".
[Admiralty Decreets, Vol.38, pp1681-1730]

"Roger Flows and others for piracy and murder against several vessels in the West Indies in 1720. Ten of them found guilty and sentenced to be hanged at Leith within the flood-mark".
[Register of the Criminal Court of the Admiralty, Vol.1, 1705-1734, pp.316-400]

The only published work in this area seems to be T.C.Wade's *"Acta Curiae Admirallatus Scotiae, 1557-1561"* **[Edinburgh, 1937]**

SCOTTISH MARITIME RECORDS

The Court of Session.

The records of this institution commence with the Acts of the Lords of Council in 1478 and continue to the present day. They include processes from 1527, acts and decrees from 1542, and productions from 1627 to 1947. As with the records of the Admiralty Court, the records are relatively difficult to deal with for our period 1600 to 1850.

The List and Index Society, however, has in their Special Series Volume 23 *"Scottish Record Office, Court of Session Productions c.1760 -1840"* which greatly facilitates access to the records. This well indexed publication is mainly concerned with business or mercantile legal cases, but as it includes aspects of international trade, therefore does cover certain maritime themes. Included are: the Leith Register of Ships 1748-1749, 1750-1751, 1751-1752, [ex CS.181/Misc.27/3]; the account book of the Lovely Mary, John Brown, shipmaster in Leith, trading with Scandinavia, the Baltic, and the east coast of England 1791-1792 [CS.239/T.14/45]; the log book of the schooner Naughton, James Black, shipmaster in Peterhead, trading around the British Isles 1814-1815 [CS.235.C.28.1]; and the books of the Irvine Codfishing Company 1753-1755 [CS.228/S.5/11].

The only other guide to the Court of Session records is the *"Index to the Court of Session Minute Books, 1739 to 1776"* researched by Alexander Murdoch on behalf of the North Carolina State Archives. The emphasis here is on links, particularly emigration, between Argyll and North Carolina, but there is maritime material such as the case of the emigrant ship the Bachelor of Leith in 1774. This guide also can be found in the SRO.

Two sample abstracts from Court of Session records are as follows:

"Decreet in Absence, Messrs Parker, Hunter and Smith, merchants in Kilmarnock, against Captain John Wood, late of the Jenny of Greenock, now in the Province of .... in America".
[General Minute Book, Court of Session, page 145, 1773-1774]

"On occasion an inventory of the household goods and capital assets which has been required in evidence survives to provide an insight into the financial standing of a seafarer. Considerable information has survived for Nicol Nicolson, a small shipowner and trader in Stornaway of the early nineteenth century - his smack the Lamlash worth £400, 4 jibs, 1 gaff topsail, 1 square sail, 1 'fly-by-night', 1 foresail and bonnet, 1 mainsail, 1 mainsail

SCOTTISH MARITIME RECORDS

tarpaulin, 2 anchors, 2 chains, 1 kedge and hawse, 1 boat ashore, 3 oars, 1 cask yellow paint, 1 of white, 5 of green, 1 of black, 2 adzes, 2 barrel for beef, 1/2 empty barrel for herring, 1 crow bar, 1 cabin ladder, 'Lamlash' signboard, 1 reel, 2 log glasses, 2 compasses, 1 telltale compass, pump gear, mooring chain, 2 long oars or 'sweeps', and 1 outrigger".

[SRO.CS96.2077]

Select Bibliography

"Scottish Record Office, Court of Session Productions c1760-1840"
   List & Index Society, [London, 1987]
"Scottish American Court Records, 1733-1783", D. Dobson, [Baltimore, 1991]

SCOTTISH MARITIME RECORDS

MUSEUMS AND ARCHIVES

Aberdeen City Archives, The Charter Room, Town House, Aberdeen. AB9 1AQ
   Tel: 01224 642121
Aberdeen Maritime Museum, Shiprow, Aberdeen. AB1 2BY
   Tel: 01224 585788
Arbroath Museum, Signal Tower, Ladyloan, Arbroath, Tel: 01241 875598
Arbuthnott Museum, St Peter Street, Peterhead. AB4 6QD
   Tel: 01779 77778
Broughty Castle Museum, St Vincent Street, Broughty Ferry, Dundee.
   Tel: 01382 23141
Buckhaven Museum, College Street, Buckhaven, Fife. Tel: 01592 260732
Buckie Drifter, Freuchny Road, Buckie, Banffshire. Tel: 01542 834646
Campbelltown Museum, Hall Street, Campbelltown, Argyll. Tel: 01586 52366
Canongate Tolbooth, Canongate, Edinburgh. Tel: 0131 4143
Dumfries & Galloway Archives, 33 Burns Street, Dumfries. DG1 2PS
   Tel: 01387 69254
RRS Discovery, Discovery Quay, Dundee. Tel: 01382 201245
Dundee City Archives, Shore Terrace, Dundee. Tel: 01382 23141
Dundee University Archives, Tower Building, Dundee. DD1 4HN
   Tel: 01382 344095
Eyemouth Museum, Auld Kirk, Market Place, Eyemouth, Berwickshire.
   TD14 5HE   Tel: 018907 50678
Findhorn Heritage Centre, Morayshire. Tel: 01309 673701
Glasgow City Archives, Mitchell Library, North Street, Glasgow. G3 7DN
   Tel: 0141 221 9600
Inverkeithing Museum, The Friary, Inverkeithing. KY11 1LS
   Tel: 01383 413344
Kirkcaldy Museum, War Memorial Gardens, Kirkcaldy. KY1 1YG
   Tel: 01592 260732]
Lossiemouth Fisheries & Community Museum, Pitgaveny St., Lossiemouth.
   IV31. Tel: 01343 813772
McLean Museum, 15 Kelly Street, Greenock. PA16 8JX
   Tel: 01475 23741
Montrose Museum, Panmure Street, Montrose. Tel: 01674 673232
Moray Record Office, The Tolbooth, Forres. IV36 0AB Tel: 01309 73617
Nairn Fishertown Museum, Laing Hall, King Street, Nairn. IV12 4PD
   Tel: 01667 53331
National Library of Scotland, George IV Bridge, Edinburgh. EH1 1EW
   Tel: 0131 2220/6662
Newhaven Heritage Museum, Newhaven Harbour, Edinburgh.
   Tel: 0131 551 4165

SCOTTISH MARITIME RECORDS

Perth & Kinross Council Archive, A.K.Bell Library, 2-8 York Place, Perth.
PH2 8EP.   Tel: 01738 444949
St Andrews University Archives, University Library, North Street, St Andrews
Tel: 01334 476161
Scottish Fisheries Museum, Harbourhead, Anstruther, Fife. KY10 3AB
Tel: 01333 310628
Scottish Institute of Maritime Studies, University of St Andrews.
Tel: 01334 476161
Scottish Maritime Museum, Harbourside, Irvine. KA12 8QE
Tel: 01294 278283
Shetland Museum, Lower Hillhead, Lerwick, Shetland. ZE1 0EL
Tel: 01595 5057
Stirling Archives, Unit 6, Burghmuir Industrial Estate, Stirling. FK7 7PY
Tel: 01786 450745
Stonehaven Tolbooth Museum, The Harbour, Stonehaven.
Tel: 01779 477778
Stromness Museum, 52 Alfred St., Stromness, Orkney. Tel: 01856 850025
The Frigate Unicorn, Victoria Dock, Dundee. DD1 3JA   Tel: 01382 200900
Wick Heritage Museum, 20 Bank Row, Wick, Caithness. KW1 5EY
Tel: 01955 3268

The range of material in the above varies considerably.   Some are strong on artifacts and others on manuscripts. The quality and quantity of manuscript material can be significant or it may be minimal, but will be of importance to some researchers directly or indirectly.

Undernoted are random selections of the type of documents which may be found in local archives.

Aberdeen City Archives

Admiralty Court Records 1730-1796
The Shipwrecked Seamen's Fund Minutes, 1829-1867
Shipping Registers, 1824-
Shore Work Accounts 1596-1680

SCOTTISH MARITIME RECORDS

Dumfries & Galloway Archives

Document re James Boyd, James and Malcolm Thomas, who had been imprisoned for refusing to sail to and from Virginia by James Corbel, shipmaster, but were subsequently releaded on caution, 13.4.1741. [DGA.GF4.20.17]

Admiralty Court minute book for the Barony of Logan and Clonyard, 1788-1806. [DGA: GGD3]

Letter from John Hair to William Johnston, mariner, re wages on the sloop Henry, 10 November 1797. [DGA:RB2.1.39]

Mariner's Register ticket made out to George Christie Irving, as a seaman, who was born at Dalbeattie 22 August 1834, issued at Liverpool 21 November 1850. [DGA:RB2.5.46]

St Andrews University Archives:

Admiralty Court Book of East Fife 1738-1775 [B3.7.2]
Anstruther Sea Box Society, Minute Book 1838-1943 [B3.7.3]
Pittenweem Sea Box Society, Minute book and accounts 1633-1840 [B3.7.4-5]
St Andrews Sea Box Society Papers 1643-1974
St Andrews Harbour Records 1771-1952 [B65.18.1-5]

Stirling Archives:

Kincardine-on-Forth Sailors Box, 1744-1821 [PD102.1-2]

SCOTTISH MARITIME RECORDS

David Dobson's Maritime Publications

The Mariners of Aberdeen and the North of Scotland, 1600-1700, pt.1
The Mariners of Aberdeen and the North of Scotland, 1700-1800, pt.1
The Mariners of Angus, 1600-1700, pt.1
The Mariners of Angus, 1700-1800, pt.1
The Mariners of Angus, 1700-1800, pt.2
The Mariners of the Clyde and Western Scotland, 1600-1700, pt.1
The Mariners of the Clyde and Western Scotland, 1700-1800, pt.1
The Mariners of Fife, 1700-1800 pt.1
The Mariners of Kirkcaldy and West Fife, 1600-1700", pt.1
The Mariners of the Lothians, 1600-1700, pt.1
The Mariners of the Lothians, 1600-1700, pt.2
The Mariners of the Lothians, 1700-1800, pt.1
The Mariners of St Andrews and the East Neuk, 1600-1700, pt.1
Scots Whalers, pre 1800, pt.1
Dundee Whalers, 1750-1850, pt.1
Tales of the Whalers
Scottish Seafarers of the Seventeenth Century
Scottish Seafarers of the Eighteenth Century

LOCH RANZA BAY,

And the manner of taking the basking Shark.

Lightning Source UK Ltd.
Milton Keynes UK
171125UK00008BA/55/P